Angels We Have Heard on High

Twelve Days of Good News for All People

David Roseberry

An RML Book (Read. Mark. Learn.)

An Imprint of LeaderWorks

Copyright © 2025 by David H. Roseberry. All rights reserved.

No portion of this book may be reproduced in any form without written permission from the publisher or author except as permitted by U.S. copyright law.

Cover Design: David Roseberry

ISBN: 979-8-9917872-1-5

+
RML BOOKS
LEADERWORKS
4545 CHARLEMAGNE DR., PLANO, TX 75024
PUBLISHED IN THE UNITED STATES OF AMERICA

❀ Formatted with Vellum

Contents

Angels We Have Heard on High	v
The Angels Proclamation	1
Fear Not!	5
The First Day of Christmas	
Behold	9
The Second Day of Christmas	
Good News	13
The Third Day of Christmas	
Great Joy	15
The Fourth Day of Christmas	
For All The People	17
The Fifth Day of Christmas	
Unto You	19
The Sixth Day of Christmas	
In the City of David	21
The Seventh Day of Christmas	
A Savior	23
The Eight Day of Christmas	
Christ the Lord	25
The Ninth Day of Christmas	
Sign to You	27
The Tenth Day of Christmas	
A Baby	29
The Eleventh Day of Christmas	
Glory and Peace	31
The Twelfh Day of Christmas	
Conclusion	33
About the Author	35
Also by David Roseberry	37

Angels We Have Heard on High
An Introduction

In November, as I hurried to finish our Advent devotions and these Christmas reflections, I found myself oddly frustrated with my spell-check. Again and again, a thin blue line appeared beneath one particular word: *manger*.

The software was certain I had made a mistake. Surely, it suggested, I meant *manager*.

Manger or **manager**.

I smiled at first. Then I paused. There may be a sermon here. Somewhere.

There was.

A manager organizes, oversees, controls.
A manager keeps things moving, makes plans, sets schedules, ensures productivity.
A manager belongs to the world as we know it.
A manager is busy, efficient, always pressing toward what comes next.

But a *manger* is something else entirely.

A manger does not manage.
It does not direct or oversee.

It simply holds.
It holds what has been given.
It waits.

Christmas has a way of teaching us how to wait.

Perhaps that is why the world keeps mistaking the manger for a manager. We are so accustomed to motion and mastery that stillness looks like a mistake. But Christmas does not ask us to manage the moment. It asks us to receive it.

The manger waits.
And in the waiting, God comes.

Christmas comes quietly, even when the world insists on being loud. It slips in through familiar melodies and small flames, through an ancient story we love but often hurry past. We know the outlines—Bethlehem, shepherds, angels—but familiarity can soften our wonder into routine.

A First Sermon

And we know this line. It is the first line of a short few phrases spoken or sung by the Christmas angels, as Luke records it:

> *"Fear not, for behold, I bring you good news of great joy that will be for all the people."*
>
> — Luke 2:10

This is the first sermon of Christmas—preached not by a priest or prophet, but by an angel sent from God. These words were meant to calm the frightened hearts of the shepherds. They did just that.

They are words intended to reframe the world and set all of history on a new course. They did that too.

This small book is an invitation to stay at the scene of the manger for just a little longer, and listen carefully to what the angels said to the shepherds just a little more intently.

Life will move on soon enough.
Work will resume.
Travel will begin.
The New Year is looming.
Your calendar will fill again.

But Luke almost begs us not to rush away. He urges us to remember the fulfillment of ancient promises and the quiet beginning of a new life in God's great world ahead.

Over the twelve days of Christmas, we will return again and again to that first sermon, taking it gently apart—word by word, phrase by phrase. Each reflection opens a small window into a vast mystery.

Read one a day, or linger longer if you wish. Wherever you find yourself, let these days keep you close to the opening scene of the most incredible story ever told.

Christmas is not something we rush through and leave behind.

It is something we receive.
It is Someone we welcome.
Come. Stay. Listen closely.

The angels are still speaking.

How to Use This Book

This book was written to be read slowly.

You may choose to read one reflection each day through the Twelve Days of Christmas, letting the angel's sermon accompany you morning by morning or night by night. You can also read it straight through, returning as often as you wish to particular words or phrases that linger in your heart.

It's short that way—about 5000 words.

Some readers will keep this book by a favorite chair. Others may place it by the bedside, or tuck it into a bag or car console as life resumes its pace. Wherever you read, allow yourself to pause.

And if you like what you read, if you are growing in your faith and wish to know more and explore more of the story of Jesus Christ, the expectations that awaited Him long ago, and the impact He has made on our world, please follow me on Substact at The Anglican, where I write regularly.

Grace and peace,

David Roseberry ☩
Christmas 2025

The Angels Proclamation

THIS SHORT PASSAGE from Luke 2 is, in effect, the first sermon of Christmas. It is shorter than most sermons preached on Christmas Eve. It is a handful of lines spoken in the dark, on an ordinary hillside, to men no one was watching. And yet these words carry more weight than all the sermons that would follow.

The words below are just two verses spoken (or sung!) to the shepherds when they wondered what had happened in the cave on the Bethlehem hillside.

We will return to these words throughout the book. Bookmark this page or dogear it. Soon, you will have memorized every word.

> *"Fear not, for behold, I bring you good news of great joy that will be for all the people. For unto you is born this day in the city of David a Savior, who is Christ the Lord. And this will be a sign for you: you will find a baby wrapped in swaddling cloths and lying in a manger."*
> And suddenly there was with the angel a multitude of the heavenly host praising God and saying,
> *"Glory to God in the highest, and on earth peace among those with whom he is pleased!"*
>
> — *Luke 2:10-12*

Over the twelve chapters of this book, you will be invited to dwell with these words. You may read one each day, letting them accompany you through the Twelve Days of Christmas. Or you may read them all at once, like a single long breath drawn in at the manger.

Either way, these lines will lead you back again and again to the moment when heaven first named what God was doing in the world.

Angels We Have Heard on High

Fear Not!
The First Day of Christmas

Fear not, for behold, I bring you good news of great joy that will be for all the people.

Fear Not

CHRISTMAS BEGINS with a word we all need, perhaps more this year than ever: *"Fear not."* The first sound that breaks the dark fields of Bethlehem is not a command to achieve, perform, or understand, but a word to steady trembling hearts.

Reflection

Fear is part of the human story. Zachariah felt it in the temple. Mary felt it in Nazareth. The shepherds feel it now beneath the glory and the heat of heaven's light. When God draws near, our frail hearts quake.

But in Scripture, fear is always met with the gentlest command. The God who shakes the mountains also stoops to calm His people: *"Fear not."*

It is the Bible's most repeated command—not because God is scolding us, but because He remembers we are dust. His reassurance comes before His explanation. God does not ask the shepherds to understand the mystery unfolding in Bethlehem.

He asks them only to trust Him.

Fear narrows life.
Fear shrinks imagination.
Fear whispers that God is far away, that the world is out of control, that we are on our own.

But Christmas declares the opposite: God has stepped into the story Himself. The world is not abandoned. The night is not empty. The silence is not the last word.

To say "Fear not" is not to deny our anxieties. It is to place them in larger hands. It is to remember that the Child born this night will one day still the storms, feed the hungry, cleanse the leper, silence the demons, and rise from the dead. In Him, fear meets its match.

The shepherds' night begins with terror, but it ends with joy. Between the two stands the voice of God saying, "Do not be afraid." Christmas is the yearly remembrance that the Lord of heaven bends low to speak peace into human fear. He comes not to overwhelm us, but to be with us.

Prayer

O Lord of perfect peace, speak again to our hearts the ancient word: Fear not. Lift our eyes from the shadows to the light of Your coming. Teach us to trust Your presence in our weakness and Your purpose in our days. Calm our troubled minds and steady our wavering spirits, that we may receive with joy the Savior born for us. Through Christ our Lord. Amen.

Behold
The Second Day of Christmas

Fear not, for behold, I bring you good news of great joy that will be for all the people.

Behold

THE ANGEL'S next word is simple but essential: *"Behold."* It is the summons to open our eyes and pay attention, for God is doing something the world has never seen.

Reflection

Scripture often calls us to behold. The prophets cry, "Behold, your God!" The psalmist urges us to "behold the beauty of the Lord." John the Baptist points and says, "Behold, the Lamb of God." To behold is more than to look; it is to awaken, to notice, to stand still long enough to receive revelation.

At Christmas, we are invited to see again—really see.

So much of life is lived on the surface, in hurry, in routine.

We skim our days.

We skim our worship.
We skim our faith.

But the angel tells the shepherds, and us, to pause long enough for wonder to break through.

"Behold" is not a suggestion. It is a gentle and gracious command. It asks us to let go of distractions, to walk slower, to light a candle and remember that the God of Abraham has entered His own world as a child.

Eternity lies wrapped in swaddling cloths.
Heaven has a heartbeat.
God's Word has taken flesh.

The shepherds had no preparation for this moment—no religious training, no theological vocabulary, no expectation that this night would be different from any other. Yet they are the first to hear the invitation. Behold. Look. Attend. A new world is being born in Bethlehem.

What might we behold this Christmas if we made room, even for a moment, to stop and look? The faithfulness of God across the years. The tenderness of His mercy. The humility of Christ. The light that shines in our darkness. The grace that meets us unprepared and unworthy.

Christmas does not ask us to create wonder. It asks us to notice it.

Prayer

Open our eyes, Lord, that we may behold the marvel of Your coming. Slow our steps, quiet our minds, and awaken our hearts to the beauty of Christ in our midst. Give us grace to see what You are doing in our lives and in the world You love. Through Jesus Christ our Lord. Amen.

Good News
The Third Day of Christmas

Fear not, for behold, I bring you good news of great joy that will be for all the people.

Good News

THE ANGEL DOES NOT BRING advice, encouragement, or inspiration. He brings *news*—a message from heaven about something God has done, not something we must do.

Reflection

The Gospel begins with an announcement. It is not a philosophy to ponder or a system to master. It is a proclamation, like the heralds who once ran across ancient cities to declare that a great victory had been won.

"Good news" is the heartbeat of the Christian faith.

Not good intentions.
Not good efforts.
Not good insights.

News. A declaration that God has acted decisively in history for us and for our salvation.

What is this news? That the long-awaited Messiah has come. That the promises given to Abraham, Moses, and David are now fulfilled. That sin will be forgiven, death defeated, the lost found, and the broken restored.

That the world is not left to its ruin but visited by its Maker.

We often treat Christianity as if it depends on our performance. But before we ever respond, before a single disciple obeys a single command, heaven announces what God has done.

Christmas is pure grace: news delivered to ordinary people in the dark, on a night they never expected to matter.

The shepherds bring nothing. They contribute nothing. They simply receive the message. That is how all faith begins—with hearing, with listening, with the humble acceptance that God has moved toward us long before we moved toward Him.

This Christmas, receive the good news again: God has acted. Salvation is His work. The Child in the manger is the proof that grace is not an idea but a person.

Prayer

Lord of the Gospel, let Your good news ring fresh in our hearts. Keep us from striving to earn what You freely give. Teach us to rest in the glad announcement that salvation has come and that Christ is born for us. Through Jesus our Savior. Amen.

Great Joy
The Fourth Day of Christmas

Fear not, for behold, I bring you good news of great joy that will be for all the people.

Great Joy

JOY IS the native language of Christmas. Not shallow cheerfulness, but the deep, steady gladness that rises wherever Christ is welcomed.

Reflection

The angel does not promise ordinary joy. He promises "great joy"—a joy large enough for every season of life. This joy does not depend on circumstances. It is rooted in the unchanging character of God and the unshakable victory of Christ.

Joy is not denial. It is not pretending everything is fine. The shepherds lived under Roman occupation, heavy taxation, and very uncertain futures. Their world was not easy. Yet heaven declares that joy—real joy—is possible because God has *entered the story*.

Why joy? Because the darkness is not final.

Because sin will not have the last word.
Because death itself will one day yield to life everlasting.
Because the God who seemed silent has spoken in the cries of a newborn child.

Joy is the inward echo of God's faithfulness. It is the soul's recognition that hope has taken flesh. It is the confidence that even in sorrow, God is weaving redemption.

Some Christmases, joy comes easily. In other years, joy feels distant. But the angel's message reminds us that joy is not something we manufacture. It is something we receive. It comes not from us, but to us.

The shepherds will soon run to Bethlehem, carrying their joy with them. Let us do the same. Let the news of Christ's birth rekindle wonder, gratitude, and the quiet assurance that God is with us.

Prayer

Giver of Joy, gladden our hearts with the news of Your Son's birth. Let His light dispel our shadows, and His presence renew our hope. Fill us with the great joy that only Christ can bring. Through Jesus Christ our Lord. Amen.

For All The People
The Fifth Day of Christmas

Fear not, for behold, I bring you good news of great joy that will be for all the people.

People

THE ANGEL WIDENS the circle of blessing with one sweeping phrase: *"...for all the people."* Christmas is personal, *but never private.*

Reflection

From the beginning, God promised that His salvation would reach the ends of the earth. Abraham was told that all nations would be blessed through his offspring. The prophets foresaw a day when the Gentiles would come to the light of God's glory. Now, in a field outside Bethlehem, heaven declares that the promise is being fulfilled.

"For all the people" overturns every expectation. The Messiah is not for one tribe, one nation, one class, or one generation. He comes for shepherds and kings, scholars and children, saints and sinners, insiders and outsiders. There is no category of person beyond the reach of His mercy.

Christmas reveals the generous heart of God. The Child of Mary is not a tribal deity or a regional savior. He is the Savior of the world. His kingdom is as wide as humanity itself.

This is good news for those who feel unworthy. Good news for those who feel forgotten. Good news for those who believe they have wandered too far from grace. Christ's arms are open wide, and His birth announces a kingdom without walls.

That is why the shepherds were the first to hear this invitation—not the powerful, not the religious elite, but those on the margins. God delights to begin with the least expected, so that His mercy may be shown to all.

This Christmas, let your heart widen with His. Remember that the gift of Christ is not just for you but for your neighbor, your family, your enemies, your community, your world.

Prayer

Lord of all nations, enlarge our hearts with Your compassion. Let the joy of Christ's birth move us outward in love, generosity, and welcome. Make us bearers of Your good news to all people. Through Jesus Christ our Lord. Amen.

Unto You
The Sixth Day of Christmas

For unto you is born this day in the city of David
a Savior, who is Christ the Lord.

Unto You

CHRISTMAS BECOMES personal with two astonishing words: *"unto you."* The angel speaks not in abstractions but in direct address.

Reflection

> *"Unto you is born this day…"*

We often read this as a general announcement, but the shepherds heard it as a direct message addressed to them—ordinary men, unknown to the world, living their quiet lives in the fields.

Christmas is the story of a God who does not remain distant. He draws near. He speaks personally. He calls each of us by name. The Child born in Bethlehem is not simply a gift to the world; He is a gift to *you*.

We sometimes imagine that God works only in the grand sweep of history, but the angel reminds us that God's work always comes down to the human heart. Salvation is not a theory. It is a relationship. Christ comes for individuals as surely as He comes for nations.

"Unto you" means:

- Your fears are seen.
- Your sins are forgiven.
- Your life matters.
- Your future is held in His hands.

The shepherds had no pedigree, no influence, no expectation of divine visitation. Yet heaven addresses them directly. Grace always moves toward the undeserving.

This Christmas, dare to believe that Christ comes for you—not only for the world, not only for the church, not only for the devout, but for you in the fullness of your story, your wounds, your hopes, and your need.

Prayer

Lord Jesus, born for the salvation of the world, let us hear the tender address of Your grace anew. Come to us, dwell with us, and let Your presence transform our hearts. Through Christ our Lord. Amen.

IN THE CITY OF DAVID
THE SEVENTH DAY OF CHRISTMAS

For unto you is born this day in the city of David a Savior, who is Christ the Lord.

IN THE CITY

BETHLEHEM IS MORE than a place on a map. It is a promise kept. Every detail of Christmas echoes the faithfulness of God.

Reflection

The angel reminds the shepherds that this birth takes place *"in the city of David."* That small phrase carries centuries of expectation. God promised David that one of his descendants would sit on the throne forever. The prophets foretold a ruler born in Bethlehem who would shepherd His people Israel.

Most kings build their identity on power. Christ builds His on promise—promises made long before His birth, kept in precise detail by a God who never forgets.

Bethlehem itself speaks. It was small, almost forgettable. Yet from this humble village comes the King of kings. God delights to bring greatness from littleness, glory from quietness, redemption from obscurity.

Our world is tempted to dismiss small things. But Bethlehem shows us that God honors them.

The small prayer.
The small act of kindness.
The small obedience.

Nothing is wasted in His kingdom. His greatest works often begin in the smallest places.

The shepherds know Bethlehem well. It is their region, their home. They have walked its paths and tended flocks near its hills. Perhaps they never imagined that the center of the world would shift into their own backyard. Yet such is the mercy of God.

This Christmas, remember that the God who works in Bethlehem also works in the small corners of your life. His promises reach even the quiet places where you feel unseen.

Prayer

Faithful God, who fulfilled Your promise in the city of David, fulfill Your purposes in us. Let the humility of Bethlehem shape our hearts and the certainty of Your promises sustain our hope. Through Jesus Christ our Lord. Amen.

A Savior
The Eight Day of Christmas

For unto you is born this day in the city of David a Savior, who is Christ the Lord.

Savior

THE ANGEL GIVES the Child His mission before giving Him His name: *He is a Savior.* Christmas is about rescue—God's rescue.

Reflection

We are not self-sufficient creatures. We cannot save ourselves. The story of Scripture, and the story of our own hearts, makes that plain. We need forgiveness, healing, restoration, and deliverance.

We need Someone strong enough to bear our burdens and gentle enough to enter our weakness.

The angel does not declare, "A helper is born," or "A teacher is born." He declares, "A Savior is born." Jesus comes not merely to inspire or guide, but to rescue—to deliver His people from sin, death, and the powers of darkness.

The shepherds likely understood "Savior" in terms of deliverance from enemies or oppression. But Christ brings a deeper liberation. He enters the world not to adjust our circumstances but to transform our condition. He takes on our humanity so that He might redeem it from the inside out.

We sometimes imagine we're beyond the need for saving. Yet Christmas reminds us that salvation is the heart of the story. If all we needed was advice, God would have sent a prophet. If all we needed was motivation, He would have sent a leader. But because we need salvation, He sent a Savior.

And He comes not reluctantly, but gladly—with mercy, with compassion, with steadfast love.

Prayer

O Savior of the world, rescue us from the sin that clings so closely and the fear that burdens our hearts. Heal us, forgive us, and make us new. Let the joy of Your salvation be born in us this Christmas. Amen.

Christ the Lord
The Ninth Day of Christmas

For unto you is born this day in the city of David
a Savior, who is Christ the Lord.

Christ the Lord

THREE TITLES FALL upon the Child in the manger: Savior, Christ, and Lord. Each reveals a dimension of His identity and His mission.

Reflection

"Christ" means "Anointed One"—the promised Messiah, the fulfillment of every hope Israel had carried through centuries of exile and expectation. To call this newborn Child "Christ" is to declare that God has kept His word.

"Lord" is even more astonishing. This is the divine title used for God Himself. The baby in the manger is not only the promised King but the eternal Lord of heaven and earth. He is both fully human and fully divine, wrapped in humility and glory at once.

In Christ, authority and gentleness meet. The One who upholds the stars now rests in Mary's arms. The One whom angels worship lies in a feeding trough. The Lord of all takes the lowest place.

Christmas demands a response.

If Jesus is Lord, then He must be more than a seasonal decoration or a sentimental memory. He claims our allegiance, our obedience, our love. He invites us into the life of His kingdom—a kingdom not of domination but of peace, truth, and grace.

To call Jesus "Lord" is both confession and comfort. It means He has authority over our lives, but also that we are never alone. The Lord who governs the universe governs our steps. His sovereignty is our safety.

Prayer

Lord Jesus Christ, King of kings and Lord of lords, reign in our hearts and rule in our lives. Let Your light dispel our darkness and Your truth guide our way. Grant that we may follow You faithfully this Christmas and always. Amen.

Sign to You
The Tenth Day of Christmas

And this will be a sign for you:
you will find a baby wrapped in swaddling cloths
and lying in a manger.

A Sign to You

GOD GIVES signs not to satisfy curiosity but to strengthen faith. The shepherds receive one of the simplest, most surprising signs in all Scripture.

Reflection

The shepherds might have expected something grand—heavenly fire, angelic glory, a royal palace. Instead, the sign is a baby wrapped in cloths and lying in a manger.

> "This will be a sign for you..."

God's signs often come in humility. He meets us in the ordinary. He hides glory beneath simplicity. The sign is not given to impress the shepherds but to reveal the character of the Savior: gentle, lowly, approachable.

The manger itself speaks. It tells us that Christ identifies with the poor, the overlooked, the vulnerable. It tells us that God's presence is not confined to the temple or the palace but found wherever He chooses to dwell—even in a stable.

The sign for the shepherds becomes a sign for us: God works in unexpected ways. He comes in humility. He draws near in weakness. He invites us to find Him where we might least expect Him.

The shepherds respond not with skepticism but with obedience. They go to see the sign for themselves. Their faith is rewarded with the sight of the newborn King.

This Christmas, pay attention to the signs God places before you—the quiet mercies, the answered prayers, the moments of peace, the nudges toward gratitude. His presence is nearer than we think.

Prayer

God of signs and wonders, open our eyes to Your presence in the humble and the ordinary. Give us faith to seek You and courage to follow where You lead. Let the manger be for us a sign of Your unfailing love. Through Christ our Lord. Amen.

A Baby
The Eleventh Day of Christmas

And this will be a sign for you:
you will find a baby wrapped in swaddling cloths
and lying in a manger.

A Baby

BETHLEHEM OFFERS us a picture of God that overturns our expectations: the Almighty enters His world as a helpless child.

Reflection

The contrast is breathtaking. The One who spoke creation into existence now sleeps in a feed trough. The Eternal becomes an infant. The Infinite becomes small.

"A baby… lying in a manger."

Why? Because God chooses humility. He comes close enough to touch, vulnerable enough to hold, gentle enough to be received without fear.

In a world obsessed with power, the manger reveals a different kind of kingdom. Christ conquers not by force but by love. He wins hearts not through domination but through compassion. The manger is the throne of a King whose glory is His humility.

The shepherds were not turned away. Neither are we.

The manger invites us all to draw near—to kneel, to wonder, to worship. Christmas bids us bring our weariness, our sin, our sorrow, and place it before the Child who came to bear it all.

The manger also reminds us that Christ is present in the lowly places of our lives. He is with us in our poverty of spirit, our brokenness, our longing. He meets us where the world least expects glory to be found.

Prayer

Lord Jesus, who chose the poverty of the manger and the weakness of infancy, grant us grace to approach You with humility and wonder. Dwell in the lowly places of our hearts, and make us instruments of Your peace. Amen.

Glory and Peace
The Twelfh Day of Christmas

Glory to God in the highest,
and on earth peace among those with whom he is pleased!

Glory and Peace

CHRISTMAS REACHES its crescendo in a song—the first carol of the Church, sung not on earth but in heaven.

Reflection

The angel's announcement suddenly becomes a choir. "A multitude of the heavenly host" fills the sky with praise. Their song is simple, stunning, eternal:

> "Glory to God in the highest, and on earth peace among those with whom He is pleased."

Glory and peace—those are the two great movements of God's salvation. Glory rises to heaven; peace descends to earth. Christmas unites the two worlds.

Glory belongs to God alone. The birth of Christ reveals His faithfulness, His humility, His love stronger than sin. The angels see the wonder of the Incarnation more clearly than we do, and they worship with overflowing joy.

Peace is His gift to us. Not merely the absence of conflict, but the restoration of the relationship—the healing of the rift between God and humanity. Peace is reconciliation, wholeness, forgiveness, and the quiet assurance that we are held securely in His mercy.

In a fractured world, this peace is priceless. It is the peace Christ will later promise to His disciples: *"My peace I give to you."* It is the peace He secures through His cross and resurrection. And it begins here, in Bethlehem, with a song.

Christmas invites us to echo the angels: to give glory to God and to receive His peace.

Prayer

God of glory and God of peace, let the song of the angels be born in our hearts. Fill us with praise for Your mighty works and grant us the peace that only Christ can give. Make our homes and our lives reflections of Your glory and Your grace. Through Jesus Christ our Lord. Amen.

Conclusion

The Song That Still Echoes

Twelve days at the manger have come and gone, yet the angel's words continue to echo across the centuries. The fields around Bethlehem have long fallen silent, the shepherds have returned to their flocks, and the Child has grown into the Savior who lived, died, and rose again.

But the message remains:

Fear not.
Behold.
I bring you good news of great joy.

Christmas is not merely a season. It is a declaration—God has come. The world is not forsaken. The darkness does not win. The King of glory has entered our humanity, taking up our weakness that we might share His life.

The manger is not the end of the story—it is the beginning. The Child wrapped in swaddling cloths is the Lord who reigns. The peace sung over Bethlehem is the peace He now gives to all who trust in Him.

May these reflections help you cherish the mystery of His coming and carry its light into the year ahead. And may the peace of Christ, born for you in the city of David, guard your heart and guide your steps until the day we join the angels' song in full.

Glory to God in the highest.

Christ is born. Alleluia.

Merry Christmas!

About the Author

David Roseberry has been an ordained Anglican minister for over 40 years. He was the founding Rector of Christ Church in Plano, Texas for over 30 years. Currently, he is the Executive Director of the non-profit ministry of LeaderWorks which serves congregations and leaders in the Anglican Church in North America. He is a preacher, bible teacher, and speaker with a growing ministry through his numerous books. Check out his Amazon Author page.

He also leads life-changing pilgrimages to Israel and other historic places of the Christian faith. Join us! Information is available at the LeaderWorks website.

He and his wife Fran live in Plano, Texas. They have five children and five grandchildren.

Stay in touch with the ministry of LeaderWorks.

Join the author as a Subscriber on Substack, where he writes regularly for a newsletter called The Anglican.

 X

Also by David Roseberry

Deepen Your Spiritual Life

The Ordinary Ways of God: Inside the Book of Ruth.

The Psalm on the Cross: A Journey to the Heart of Jesus through Psalm 22.

When the Lord is My Shepherd: Finding Hope in a Hard Time.

The Giving Life: Why it is More Blessed to Give than to Receive.

The First 24: One Man. One Mission. One Day — Jesus of Nazareth

Way Truth Life: 31 Days in the Chapter 14 of the Gospel of John

Books about Leadership

Giving Up: How Giving to God Renews Hearts, Changes Minds, and Empowers Ministry.

A Field Guide for Giving: Increasing Generosity in the Local Church

Inspiring Generosity: The 10-Step Program for Highly Successful Annual Stewardship Campaigns

The Rector, the Vestry, and the Bishop

The Seven Tools: Rediscover Your Church's Hidden Potential for Growth and Vitality

If you have questions or suggestions about this book or any others, please contact me at David@LeaderWorks.org. All of these titles are available at bulk rate discounts by contacting me.

www.ingramcontent.com/pod-product-compliance
Lightning Source LLC
Chambersburg PA
CBHW070749050426
42449CB00010B/2398